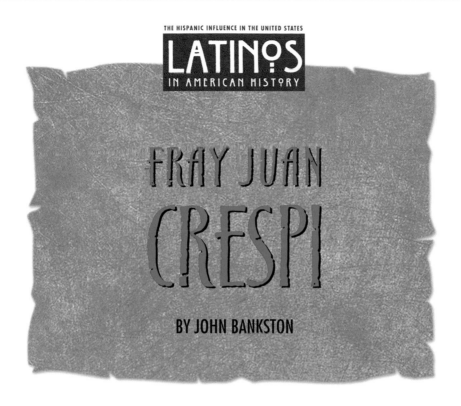

THE HISPANIC INFLUENCE IN THE UNITED STATES

LATINOS
IN AMERICAN HISTORY

FRAY JUAN CRESPI

BY JOHN BANKSTON

Mitchell Lane
PUBLISHERS

P.O. Box 196
Hockessin, Delaware 19707

THE HISPANIC INFLUENCE IN THE UNITED STATES

LATINOS
IN AMERICAN HISTORY

OTHER TITLES IN THE SERIES

Visit us on the web: www.mitchelllane.com
Comments? email us: mitchelllane@mitchelllane.com

THE HISPANIC INFLUENCE IN THE UNITED STATES

LATINOS
IN AMERICAN HISTORY

FRAY JUAN
CRESPI

BY JOHN BANKSTON

Mitchell Lane
PUBLISHERS

Printing   1   2   3   4   5   6   7   8   9

Library of Congress Cataloging-in-Publication Data

Bankston, John, 1974-
 Fray Juan Crespi / by John Bankston.
   p. cm. — (Latinos in American history)
 Summary: Profiles Fray Juan Crespi, who founded the Mission San Carlos Borromeo in Carmel by the Sea, California, and recorded his experiences as a Franciscan missionary and a member of a team of explorers.
 Includes bibliographical references and index.
 ISBN 1-58415-198-6 (lib. bdg.)
 1. Crespì, Juan, 1721-1782—Juvenile literature. 2. Explorers—California—Biography—Juvenile literature. 3. Explorers—Spain—Biography—Juvenile literature. 4. Franciscans—California—Biography—Juvenile literature. 5. Mission San Carlos Borromeo (Carmel, Calif.)—History—Juvenile literature. 6. Missions, Spanish—California—History—18th century—Juvenile literature. 7. California—Discovery and exploration—Spanish—Juvenile literature. 8. Pacific Coast (North America)—Discovery and exploration—Spanish—Juvenile literature. [1. Crespì Juan, 1721-1782. 2. Explorers. 3. Missionaries. 4. Mission San Carlos Borromeo (Carmel, Calif.)—History. 5. Missions—California. 6. Indians of North America—Missions—California. 7. California—History—To 1846.] I. Title. II. Series.
 F864.C92B36 2003
 979.4'02'092--dc21
 [B]

                    2002153058

ABOUT THE AUTHOR: Born in Boston, Massachussetts, John Bankston began publishing articles in newspapers and magazines while still a teenager. Since then, he has written over two hundred articles, and contributed chapters to books such as *Crimes of Passion*, and *Death Row 2000*, which have been sold in bookstores across the world. He has written numerous biographies for young adults, including *Mandy Moore* and *Alexander Fleming and the Story of Penicillin* (Mitchell Lane). He currently lives in Portland, Oregon.

PHOTO CREDITS: Cover: East Contra Costa Historical Society; p. 6 Monterey County Historical Society; p. 9 Archivo Iconografico, S.A./Corbis; p. 12 North Wind Picture Archive; p. 14 Collection of The Corcoran Gallery of Art/Corbis; p. 17 Robert Holmes/Corbis; p. 18 Bob Krist/Corbis; p. 20 East Contra Costa Historical Society; p. 24 Hulton/Archive; p. 26 North Wind Picture Archive; p. 34 James A. Sugar/Corbis; p. 40 Darrell Gulin/Corbis

PUBLISHER'S NOTE: This story is based on the author's extensive research, which he believes to be accurate. Some parts of the text might have been created by the author based on his research to illustrate what might have happened years ago, and is solely an aid to readability for young adults.

  The spelling of the names in this book follow the generally accepted usage of modern day. The spelling of Spanish names in English has evolved over time with no consistency. Many names have been anglicized and no longer use the accent marks or any Spanish grammar. Others have retained the Spanish grammar. Hence, we refer to Hernando De Soto as "De Soto," but Francisco Vásquez de Coronado as "Coronado." There are other variances as well. Some sources might spell Vásquez as Vazquez. For the most part, we have adapted the more widely recognized spellings.

CONTENTS

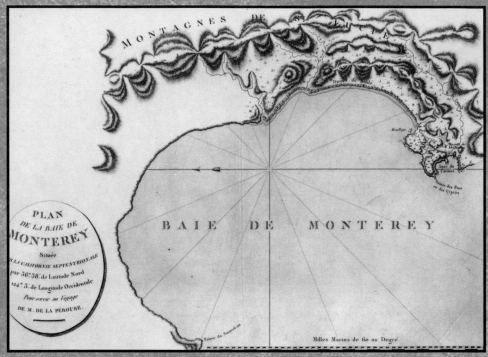

Early maps were often very inaccurate; explorers used them at their own risk. Maps such as this one of Monterey Bay lacked detail — often men like Sergeant José Ortega wound up miles from their original destination.

LUCKY ACCIDENTS

The men were starving. Every day their supplies dwindled. For weeks they survived on tortillas, nothing but tortillas. Soon the men under the command of Captain Gaspar de Portolá (gahs-PAR-day-port-oh-LA) would be eating their mules. Things looked grim.

Even worse was the sense of defeat. The primary goal of their exploration was finding Monterey Bay. The body of water could serve as port, helping the Spanish in their never-ending quest to extend their holdings. Unfortunately a previous explorer's directions were way off. So now, cold and hungry in the late fall of 1769, the party continued north, farther and farther from their base in San Diego.

Sometime in early November, chief scout Sergeant José Francisco de Ortega was sent on ahead. Accompanied by his best men, he crested the hills above Half Moon Bay and peered out into the distance. And then he saw it: an enormous bay, too large to be Monterey. What Ortega didn't know was that he and his group were the first Europeans to view what would become one of the most famous landmarks on the West Coast. They had discovered San Francisco Bay.

Trailing behind Ortega's crew, a kindly middle-aged priest looked out upon the waters and made an important declaration. The bay was large enough, he noted, that all the navies of all the countries of the world could safely nestle in its harbor.

The priest's observation would provide the suffering soldiers with neither food nor warmth. However, the bay would become an essential Spanish port, and it enabled the Spanish to develop much of California in the 18th and 19th centuries. Even more surprising, its discovery was a complete accident. Then again, most of the important discoveries in the New World were accidental.

The New World—these three little words held a magical meaning for Europeans. The lands of what would be known as North America (the United States, Canada, and Mexico) offered the promise of unexplored, unconquered territory, and above all wealth for anyone brave enough to risk the dangerous voyage across the Atlantic. After the early explorations of men like Christopher Columbus, Juan Ponce de León, and Juan Rodríguez Cabrillo, by the 1700s the territories of the New World provided unrivaled opportunities for countries such as France, England, and Spain.

Of course Europeans weren't the first people on the continent. During the Ice Age, a period tens of thousands of years ago when temperatures across the globe plummeted and tundra covered much of the planet, ancient settlers migrated to North America. Back then a thin strip of land known as Beringia ran over what is now the Bering Strait. Beringia offered a land bridge for primitive people who traveled from Asia to North America and eventually lived throughout much of the continent.

When European explorers arrived, other people had already lived in the New World for thousands of years. Beginning in the late 15th century and for the next three hundred years, Europeans slowly pushed westward, driving many of these native peoples from their homes. The United States, which began as 13 colonies bordered on the west by the Appalachian mountain range, had doubled in size by 1803.

Although the eastern United States was developed primarily by the French and English, the far western reaches of the continent—Oregon, California, and Washington—were discovered and protected by the Spanish. This area was one

Like many early discoveries, Christopher Columbus's discoveries were accidental. All he wanted was a route to the East Indies; instead he found the New World.

of the last regions to join the United States. Before it did, many of the native peoples who lived in the West suffered greatly.

In many ways the story of the United States is a story of conquest. Christopher Columbus never meant to reach North America. His voyage was the result of poor maps, poor planning, and ignorance. After his arrival in 1492, he built settlements in the Dominican Republic; about 70 years later St. Augustine was established in what is now Florida. By the early 1700s the Spanish, the French, the English, and also the Russians were in a race to establish their own settlements in North America.

But the story of territorial conquest is only a part of the story of North America.

In the southwestern portions of North America, the soldiers, settlers, and explorers were joined by another group of men. They were missionaries, and their goals were based in Catholicism. They too dreamed of conquest, but for minds and souls, not land.

In the 21st century, some people regard missionary work as coercive—forcing native peoples to adopt unfamiliar religions. Others, however, view it as noble. Missionaries today continue to venture into dangerous regions across the globe, and some have even lost their lives in places like the Philippines and Colombia. For centuries these men and women have done much more than proselytize. Hundreds of years ago Spanish missionaries not only preached their religious beliefs, but also taught the Indians new farming methods and how to read and write; they even protected them from Spanish soldiers.

Some said a single priest was worth more than a thousand soldiers. Spain began believing in this theory shortly after the bloody activities of the conquistadores, Spanish soldiers who seized land for their monarch by overpowering and killing native peoples in places like Florida and Guatemala.

In 1540 the efforts of a humble Dominican priest named Fray Luis Cancer began to change the way things had been done. Even as Spanish soldiers were fighting and dying in Florida, Cancer was traveling unharmed through Mexico. He went south into Guatemala, which was then called "the Land of War" because of its protective inhabitants who killed anyone else who tried to settle there. Cancer turned the area into Vera Paz, the Land of True Peace.

His methods were simple: Instead of the brutality of the conquistadores, he gained the trust of the native people with kind words and gifts of beads. "Deeds are love and gifts shatter rocks," he once wrote, explaining how the things he did to help the native people and the things he said were more effective than any weapon.

Unfortunately it was Spanish brutality that prematurely ended Fray Cancer's peaceful missions. During a journey to Tampa, he met up with Florida natives who'd already been devastated by conquistador Hernando de Soto's savage methods. Although the native people accepted him and his fellow priests in the beginning, after a few days they were killed. Fray Cancer was clubbed to death on the shoreline while sailors and soldiers watched in horror from a nearby boat.

Despite setbacks, Spain increasingly relied on the power of the priest. In the 17th century, after a revolt led by Pueblo El Pope drove the Spanish from New Mexico, Spain sent in Diego de Vargas and his soldiers. The Spanish eventually succeeded in reconquering New Mexico, but there were many lives lost on both sides. Spanish leaders realized there were better methods of controlling newly discovered territories. While they continued to set up forts—called

Some say a priest was worth one thousand soldiers. They helped educate the native people and taught them valuable farming skills. This illustration shows a priest preaching to Native Americans.

presidios—in places like New Mexico and Texas, on the west coast the Spanish established missions. Developed around a mission church and usually close to presidios, these settlements included schools, government buildings, living quarters, and farmland. And instead of battling the native peoples, Spain sent missionaries to work with them and win them over.

Many times Spanish missionaries were the first Europeans to come into contact with Indians, who were, as the first Spanish viceroy in Mexico Antonio de Mendoza noted, "well disposed to receive the friars, while they flee from us as [deer] fly in the forest." Because members of orders like the Franciscans and the Jesuits could travel alone into territory where soldiers were seen as threatening, the missionaries were able to establish settlements and gain the Indians' trust. Men like Junípero Serra established missions and claimed the land for Spain. These missions provided Spain with its first real toehold on the West Coast, even as the colonists established communities on the East.

Missionaries were among the first Europeans to see much of what would become the western cities we know today— places like San Diego and Los Angeles. A missionary was the one who noted the incredible potential of San Francisco Bay. While several missionaries were responsible for the exploration and settlements in these areas, one man's record of their journey describes the challenges they faced. He wrote about the first time Europeans saw what would be Los Angeles, San Francisco Bay, and La Brea Tar Pits. More than great stories, his writings provided a roadmap for future explorers and settlers.

He was a missionary. He was a writer. He was Fray Juan Crespí, and his story is a different story of America.■

Like many of our country's founders, George Washington's life was well-documented. The lives of Latinos who contributed to the development of North America are less described — the journals of Fray Juan Crespí offer insights into the obstacles faced by men like Gaspar de Portolá, and Junípero Serra.

THE
ORDER

In the 1700s there were no cameras, no radio broadcasts, no video news reports. The only record of that time are the words and drawings of the men and women who lived in it. By reading their journals and studying the maps they drew, we can learn about their lives and the work they did. Some of the founders of our country—men like Thomas Jefferson, Benjamin Franklin, and George Washington— have had their lives well documented in their own writings and in the words of their peers.

However, on the West Coast the details of many Latinos who contributed to the development of the United States are less well known. What we know of their lives is filled with gaps, like missing pages in a history book, and biographers must piece together what their lives must have been like.

The life of Fray Juan Crespí is one of these mysteries. While Crespí carefully documented the deeds of others, his own early years are largely unknown. He was born in early

1721 on the island of Majorca. The largest island of the Balearic chain, Majorca rests in the Mediterranean near the coast of Spain. With a temperate climate and rolling green hills, it offered a pleasant environment in which to grow up. Scarcely changed by progress, the island's residents earn their living today much as they did in Crespí's time—by fishing or by farming the island's many orchards and vineyards. Indeed in the 21st century, the Majorcans' colorful clothing is largely unchanged from when Crespí was a boy.

For many of the island's residents, only one thing was more important than farming and fishing: the Catholic Church. Religious life wasn't just attending Sunday services, it informed every choice and decision made not only by the people but by the Spanish government, which exercised extraordinary power over them. Three hundred years ago there was no greater honor for a family than for their son to become a priest. Catholic men who felt the calling to enter the priesthood joined monasteries, which were then called convents (both priests and nuns joined convents in the 18th century).

As a teenager Crespí pledged his life to a Catholic religious order known as the Franciscans. Named after its founder and patron saint, St. Francis of Assisi, the Franciscan Order called on those who joined not only to take the usual vows of poverty, chastity, and humility, but also to devote themselves to nature. Franciscans believed in not hurting animals and rode on mules or horses only when the distances were too far to walk. Many of them did not eat meat.

It was not an easy lifestyle, nor was it an easy time. The dark days of the Spanish Inquisition when the Catholic leadership was responsible for the torture and even murders of nonbelievers were over. However the church was still a strict and forbidding organization. The Franciscans were regular practitioners of self-flagellation: flogging themselves with whips, banging heavy stones into their chest, or enduring similar torments to banish sinful thoughts.

Despite the sacrifices, becoming a member of an order like the Franciscans also meant an education: Just being able to read and write set many of the priests apart from their peers. This talent would come in handy when Crespí left Spain.

Some of Crespí's experiences are seen reflected in the life of Junípero Serra. Eight years Crespí's senior, Serra's life

Junípero Serra was as important to western exploration as the Spanish soldiers he traveled with. His life is far better documented than Fray Juan Crespí's partly because Crespí wrote so much about him.

Born in Majorca, Juan Crespí entered the Convent of Jesus located in the capital city of Palma, shown here. In many ways, the island is unchanged from the time when Crespi lived there.

is better documented in part because Crespí wrote so much about him. Like Crespí, Serra entered the Convent of Jesus in Majorca's capital city of Palma. He was sixteen when he took his vows. After becoming a priest in 1737, he began teaching philosophy and theology (the study of faith and religion) at the prestigious University of Palma. Crespí was one of Serra's star students. Fellow student Francisco Palóu described Crespí by saying, "Besides being a very exemplary and humble friar, for I knew him since he was a boy, as we were reared together and studied together from the first rudiments until we finished theology, he was highly regarded among all his fellow pupils for his mystic and perfect religion."

Besides his humbleness and "perfect" religion, Crespí was a talented writer, so it is not surprising that he was one of the young men Serra chose to accompany him to the New World. He was the perfect person to record the Franciscans' experiences. By the middle of the 18th century, missions were becoming established in North America, primarily in Mexico. Serra was called upon to work at the Missionary College of San Fernando in Mexico City, teaching both missionaries and the native peoples there.

The risks were enormous, but Franciscans were trained to accept sacrifices. On August 30, 1749, Serra and Crespí, along with Palóu and over two dozen other Franciscans and Dominicans, boarded a ship bound for the New World. The journey was a dangerous gamble, but surviving the passage would be the least of their challenges.■

For Franciscans, only the most difficult journeys made it permissible to travel by mule. Here Fray Juan Crespí and military leader Don Pedro Fages contemplate the challenging terrain.

DANGEROUS PASSAGE

All voyages across the ocean in the middle 1700s were treacherous. Large portions of the Atlantic were uncharted, and weather was unpredictable. But just surviving the tumultuous ocean was only part of the challenge. The trip took several months, and 18th-century sailors didn't have the ability to store food like we do today. Citrus fruits in particular—lemons, oranges, and the like—were unavailable. Because of this, many of the men suffered from scurvy. This disease is caused by a lack of vitamin C, a nutrient found in citrus fruits. Scurvy causes bleeding under the skin and extreme weakness; it can even be fatal. In later years, arriving in California or Florida with its abundant citrus trees was like reaching the Promised Land.

Yet as dangerous as transatlantic crossings were in the 1700s, the ninety-nine-day journey made by Juan Crespí and his fellow Franciscans in 1749 stood out. During the passage the captain, an English Protestant, threatened to throw the Spanish Catholics overboard. He even put a knife to Serra's throat. The humble priest took his threats seriously and began wearing a wooden cross nearly half his five-foot height.

Just as the ship finally reached the fringes of the Gulf of Mexico, a violent storm arose. The small craft was battered by wind and water; the priests' prayers became especially fervent. When they managed to reach the eastern coast of Mexico, the Franciscans surely were convinced it was their prayers that had kept them alive.

Over the previous century the Spanish had established missions across Mexico. While reaching the western shores meant a difficult overland journey, it was still easier than sailing around the tip of South America or trekking over Panama—a less favorable option still used in the 18th century.

While Juan Crespí's trip to the Apostolic College of San Fernando was difficult, it didn't compare to the challenges faced by his former teacher. Junípero Serra chose to travel as St. Francis had—by foot, carrying no provisions and relying on God and begging to supply his needs. While Serra survived, a spider or insect bite inflicted during the 270-mile journey left his leg so damaged that it would trouble him for the rest of his life. Despite his pain, he rarely traveled by mule or horse.

Crespí also rarely rode, but in circumstances like the trip to Mexico City, he went—perhaps wisely—by donkey. He arrived in a few weeks, none the worse for wear, at the College of San Fernando. The educational institution was responsible for preparing all the Spanish priests who chose to become North American missionaries. The education was partly religious training, partly a preparation for exploring and surviving in unknown territory.

At the college, Father Serra was given the directorship of the Novice Master, an important post. Even with the honor, he lived simply, as did the rest of the Franciscans. As the missionaries began working at the college, Crespí devoted much of his time to working with the native peoples who lived around the small community of Mexico City. He studied their languages and eventually became fluent in several dialects. Being able to speak their language was the first step in introducing them both to Catholicism and to European farming techniques, which greatly improved the quantity and quality of the food they produced.

Five months after their arrival, Crespí, Palóu, and Serra traveled almost 200 miles north to the Sierra Gorda Mission. There Serra became the leader of the small community of priests, while Crespí continued to work with the locals, who'd had little contact with Europeans.

Father Crespí stayed there with Father Serra until 1758, when they were called back to the College of San Fernando. Father Serra's methods of getting the Indians' attentions were, to say the least, impressive. One incident was so dramatic that Father Palóu, despite being familiar with the techniques of self-flagellation, recorded it in great detail: "[Serra] took out a chain and lowering his habit so as to uncover his back, having exhorted his followers to penance, he began to scourge himself so violently that the entire congregation broke into tears." After viewing this, Palóu recalled, another man walked to the pulpit, took the chain from Serra's hands, then walked over to the highest part of the church. Once there he began to imitate Serra's blows. "So violent and merciless were the strokes that, before the whole congregation, he fell to the floor. . . . After he received the last Sacraments where he fell, he died."

In 1768 Serra was appointed President of Baja Missions, the settlements that had been established on the strip of

Paranoid that Jesuit priests might overthrow him, King Carlos III expelled them from their Mexican missions. The move allowed Franciscans like Crespí to flourish.

land now known as Baja California, or Lower California. Back then the area we now know as the state of California was called Alta, or Upper, California. The territory had been largely unexplored and lacked any settlements.

Serra didn't get his posting because of his years of religious service. He got it because back home the leaders of Spain realized Russian exploration was about to become a threat. They needed missionaries like Crespí and Serra to establish settlements along the western coast of North America before the Russians did.

By then, Franciscans were favored over the Jesuits by Spain. In 1767 the Spanish king, Carlos (or Charles) III believed the Jesuits were a threat to his rule. He was convinced they were plotting to assassinate him. That summer he expelled the Jesuits from Mexico, forcing them to leave with only their prayer books. Many died on the journey. The Franciscans were the only priests King Carlos III trusted to establish the missions in Alta California.

It was exciting work in an exciting time. Crespí was about to become a true explorer: meeting new peoples, taking ships and land routes across areas of North America unseen by Europeans. By then the period of war and violent conquest was over; Crespí and his fellow missionaries enjoyed a span of relative peace. Their missions led to more successful explorations than had occurred under the crusading conquistadores, as Spain truly recognized the value of the cross over the sword.

Although the established settlements were relatively calm places, the unexplored territories were seething with potential dangers. Fray Juan Crespí was about to experience those dangers firsthand. ■

Gaspar de Portolá conducted significant explorations into the western region surrounding what would become San Diego. As the trip's recorder, Fray Juan Crespí made careful note of how difficult the trek was.

CHAPTER 4

BY LAND AND BY SEA

The threat to Spain didn't come from the English or from the French. Those countries were too busy dealing with problems on the East Coast. For decades, Spain's interest in North America had been on the wane. Although they'd planned on mounting explorations and building settlements in Alta California, for over 200 years Spain was too concerned about money problems at home to worry about their New World settlements.

The Russians changed everything.

In 1724 Captain Vitus Bering began his explorations of the strait that would later bear his name. Like Columbus, Bering's initial goals and his eventual accomplishments were very different: Bering's discovery was also an accident.

Russia's leader, Czar Peter the Great, sent Bering on a quest to find a northern route from the Pacific to the Atlantic Ocean. Instead, he sailed into the Arctic. During the voyage the captain discovered the Bering Strait, an area where Russia's Siberia and what would become Alaska were separated by only a few miles of icy water.

Bering brought back maps and valuable sea otter skins to Mother Russia, and soon his countrymen followed the path he'd cut. Over the next few decades Russians established settlements on Bering, Unalaska, and other islands that extended down the Alaskan coast for nearly a thousand miles. Russian ships also began cruising along the Washington and Oregon coastline.

Spain was nervous.

On January 23, 1768, the Spanish government issued direct orders to leaders in Mexico: "The High Government of Spain being informed of the repeated attempts of a foreign nation upon the northern coasts of California with aims by no means favorable to the Monarchy and its interests [the governor of California and his men] should take effective measures to guard that part of his dominions from invasion and insult."

The mission would involve soldiers and missionaries. General José de Gálvez would lead the soldiers, Serra would lead the missionaries, and Crespí would record it all.

The group left in early 1769 in two divisions. The first traveled by boat along the Pacific. The pair of ships, the *San Antonio* and the *San Carlos*, along with a supply ship named the *San José*, made the ocean journey from Velicatá in northern Baja California to the area around San Diego.

The second division went overland, leaving in the spring. Crespí made the 400-mile journey by foot, accompanied by Captain Rivera and soldiers he described as "the finest horsemen in the world." It was a difficult trek. In a letter to Fray Palóu, Crespí wrote, "I do not know how to tell your Reverence what we suffered from hunger on this journey, because the captain brought only sixteen [containers] of very old flour and ten packs of jerked beef. . . . We had two meals a day of poor tortillas which were mostly bran, and a bit of roast beef that was so hard and so salty that only necessity could make one eat it."

Although the first eight days of the trip were made along a route already mapped and explored by another priest, the remainder of the journey was into unknown territory. Much of the time the weather was cold and rainy. The men traveled in wet garments, struggling against the terrain. Forty native men accompanied them, using shovels and pickaxes to clear through the forest. Protecting them all were over two dozen cuirassiers, or leather-jacket soldiers, so called because of their thick, sleeveless leather armor that could protect them against arrows.

On June 30 the group could see in the distance the masts of ships. The next day explorer Gaspar de Portolá, Crespí, and the rest of the men reached San Diego. Crespí carefully recorded his impressions, writing, "All the port is well populated with a large number of villages of Indians, too clever, wide-awake and business like for any Spaniard to get ahead of them. The men are naked and almost all are very much painted. They are well armed with bows and quivers of arrows." While their weapons may have made them look forbidding, the Indians allowed the group to begin establishing the first missions in San Diego. It was Crespí who planted the large cross marking the territory for Spain, leaving at its wooden base a bottle containing the legal document claming the region for his country.

Despite the hardships he'd endured, Crespí's journey was easier than the one made by those who went by boat. Because of mapping errors, the ships sailed too far north and had to double back to reach the port. It took 54 days for the *San Antonio* to land at San Diego and 110 days for the *San*

Carlos. By then the men on board were so sick from scurvy that they were unable to lower the rowboats to take them to shore.

The *San José* was lost at sea.

Serra, who'd followed the land route carved by the native peoples, reached San Diego on the last day of June. There was a great celebration, but their joy was tempered by tragedy. Over 90 men had died on the *San Carlos*, and many more from the *San José*.

Serra stayed in San Diego, organizing the mission. Portolá took Crespí and nearly 70 others on the next leg of the exploration. They continued north, seeking the large and sheltered bay described by a Spanish explorer over a century earlier.

During the fall of 1602, Sebastián Vizcaíno (viz-ky-EE-no) had spent his own money to take three ships—the *San Diego*, the *Santo Tomás*, and the *Tres Reyes*—on a trip up the western coast of Mexico. He hoped to expand on an earlier and ill-fated exploration managed by Juan Rodríguez Cabrillo.

Instead his trip was equally difficult. The men faced everything from leaking water barrels to scurvy. Although Vizcaíno was able to reach the bay Cabrillo had called San Miguel (at which point Vizcaíno renamed it San Diego Bay), his trip farther north was nothing but trouble. Scurvy forced him to send 34 men back to Mexico (only 9 of whom survived the journey), and the northwest winds battered the tiny vessels.

On January 3, 1603, Vizcaíno and his men traveled nine miles over challenging hills before reaching Monterey Bay. The trip was considered a success.

Although he was a decent explorer, Vizcaíno gave lousy directions.

On August 2, 1769, Crespí's group traveled through the area of Elysian Park in what would become Los Angeles. After the difficult trip, the area must have seemed especi- blessed.

"After traveling about a league and a half through a pass between low hills, we entered a very spacious valley," Crespí wrote in his journal, "well grown with cottonwoods and alders, among which ran a beautiful river from north-north-west and then doubling at the point of a steep hill, it went on afterward to the south. As soon as we arrived about eight [Indians] from a good village came to visit us; they live in this delightful place among the trees on the river."

Instead of the hostile tribes the Spanish feared, Crespí described one group of Indians that offered the men their land if they would stay, promising to

"feed us on chia and other seeds and that they would build us homes and protect us. We told them that if we returned we would stay with them and that we would make a house for God and afterwards one for ourselves and that we would clothe them and plant for them and also defend them from their enemies. When we said this to the one who was captain of them all, he shed tears of happiness and joy."

It was Portolá who gave the river its name: El Rio de Nuestra Señora la Reina de los Angeles de Porciúncula, or the River of Our Lady the Queen of the Angels of the Small Portion. Eventually both the river and the city through which it flowed had their names shortened to Los Angeles.

The next day Crespí and the rest of the men were given a true California welcome: three minor earthquakes. Despite the excitement, Crespí would note, "it has good land for planting all kinds of grains and seed and is the most suitable site of all we have seen for a mission, for it has all the requisites for a large settlement."

After their adventure with the earthquakes, the group reached another Los Angeles landmark—La Brea Tar Pits. "Marshes of a certain substance like pitch, they were boiling and bubbling and the pitch came out mixed with an abundance of water," Crespí wrote, describing an area that would do more than yield a bunch of ice-age fossils in the early 1900s. The tar pits would also reveal the first hint of oil in the New World.

After leaving the Los Angeles area, the group continued their trip north. There the land route became nearly impassable, as "the mountains . . . are inaccessible not only for men but also for goats and deer," Crespí explained in his journal. The trip over the Santa Lucia Mountain Range proved so demanding that it "was a sad spectacle for us poor wayfarers, tired and worn out by the fatigue of a long journey. . . . All this tended to oppress our hearts; but remembering the object to which these toils were directed, and that it was for the greater glory of God through the conversion of souls and for the service of the king, whose dominions were being enlarged by this expedition, all were animated to work cheerfully."

Their efforts paid off—but not right way.

Finding Monterey Bay based on Vizcaíno's maps was proving impossible. Worse, the men were starving (on the trip home the mules would become a prime source for dinner).

Exhausted, the group continued north. That's when luck struck. They'd decided to take a different route than the one Vizcaíno's maps indicated. Because they did, they found a bay much larger than the one at Monterey. "In a word, it is a very large and fine harbor," Crespí wrote in a letter to

Palóu about the discovery, "such that not only all the navy of our most Catholic Majesty but those of all Europe could take shelter in it."

Crespí was the first missionary to see San Francisco Bay. On the same trip, he also discovered Palo Alto, now the location of Stanford University.

Crespí's record of the trip would provide a guide for future explorations and eventually convince many to risk settling along the West Coast, "From San Diego to that port [San Francisco]," Crespí wrote, "which is the farthest which this land expedition reached, I may say that all the land in general is everywhere well wooded, has abundant forage and countless other kinds of herbage and of its own accord produces as food for the numerous Indians' plentiful harvests… All this land is populated with a large number of Indians who are very gentle, generous and well formed."

When Crespí returned to Mexico, he became the only priest to make the 1,500-mile march from Velicatá to San Francisco and back. The trail established by Portolá and described by Crespí would become El Camino Real ("the King's Highway"), a very important road for California travelers, and one that still exists.

But Crespí's explorations weren't over. Not by a long shot. ■

The San Carlos Borroméo mission in Carmel was established in 1771 by Junípero Serra. It would be the official capital for Alta and Baja California for the next fifty years.

CALM IN CARMEL

T he Portolá expedition, recorded by Fray Juan Crespí, was enormously successful. Besides their discovery of San Francisco Bay, the men encountered a gigantic new tree they called *palo colorado*. It was the first time Europeans had seen the impressive redwoods that were abundant along the northern portions of Alta California.

Before returning to San Diego, the group planted two large white crosses, with glass jars holding legal documents at their base. The crosses at the shoreline of San Francisco Bay did more than claim the territory for Spain, they represented the first step toward future missions.

In San Diego, life was not so promising.

Since Crespí's departure, over 50 men had died from either illness or hunger. The rest just wanted to go home. Some of the Indians had stolen provisions from them; the rest of their supplies were severely depleted. Starvation was a very real possibility. Serra refused to give up.

"What I have desired least is provisions," Serra wrote. "Our needs are many, it is true; but if we have health, a tortilla and some vegetables, what more do we want? If I see that along with food hope vanishes, I shall remain with Father Juan Crespí and hold out to the last breath."

Hope did not give out. The *San Antonio,* which had left for Mexico months before, returned heavy with provisions. The northern journey continued for the two priests as Serra boarded the *San Antonio* and Crespí went over the land route.

On June 3, 1770, the pair founded the Mission San Carlos Borroméo at Monterey. "After preparing the altar and hanging the bells from the branches of the tree," Serra wrote, "we sang the hymn 'Veni, Creator,' and blessed the holy water. We then raised aloft and blessed a great cross, likewise the royal standards. After that, I celebrated the first mass."

Finding San Carlos Borroméo too far from the protection of the presidio, Serra had the mission moved in 1771 to the scenic coastal area now known as Carmel-by-the-Sea, which is on the Monterey Peninsula along Carmel Bay. In 1777 it would become the official capital of both Baja and Alta California, and it would remain so for the next 50 years. With its temperate climate and pristine landscape, the area was ideal for a mission. It would become the home base for Crespí and Serra during the last decade of their lives.

Back in Mexico and Spain, the efforts of the priests and soldiers were celebrated by "a general ringing of the bells of the cathedral and all the other churches in order that all might realize the importance of the Port of Monterey to the Crown of our monarch and also to give thanks for the happy success of the expeditions," Crespí wrote. "For by their means the dominion of our king had been extended by over three hundred leagues of good land."

Although Crespí wrote that converting the Indians and teaching them farming techniques took much longer than the Spaniards expected, by the 1780s six thousand of them would be converted to Catholicism. Most of the neophytes lived and worked around the newly established missions in Alta California. Crespí worked alongside Serra as the two not only converted the Indians but also trained them to be farmers, ranchers, and builders. As he noted in his diary, because of their efforts, the Alta missions would eventually support 15,000 head of animals such as sheep and cattle, while the nearby fields yielded more than 15,000 bushels of grains such as wheat.

All of this was accomplished in just over 10 years after Crespí reached San Diego.

Besides educating the Indians in European farming methods, Crespí and Serra also worked hard to protect them from Spanish soldiers. It wasn't easy. Sometimes they had to invoke the authority of the Catholic Church, convincing soldiers to release Indians the missionaries believed had been wrongly imprisoned. Crespí also tried, somewhat unsuccessfully, to shelter the Indian women from the soldiers' attentions.

In a letter home, Serra complained that one of the military commanders, Don Pedro Fages, "considers himself as absolute and that the missionaries count for less than the least of his soldiers, so that the missionaries cannot speak to him on the slightest matter concerning the missions." Despite Fages's attitude, Crespí and Serra never hesitated to speak up when they believed the Indians were being poorly treated.

Although Crespí was very involved with most of the nine missions Serra founded in Alta California, the scribe's days of exploration weren't over. For while Carmel-by-the-Sea continued to be his home, during the last 12 years of his life he often left the area.

Crespí conducted a mule train for "starving San Diego." Upon arriving, he reported, "I found few victuals. There were only seven [containers] of corn and about two hundred pounds of flour. The guards for a long time maintained themselves with half a pint of corn and only twenty ounces of flour a day; the fathers likewise, with little milk. They say that thus they have passed most of the year, without lard, without tallow, without even a candle of this kind, and even without wine for the Holy Masses."

Crespí's provisions helped; so too did the arrival of the *San Carlos* and *San Antonio* in August of 1772. Even with the help, San Diego's desert location meant frequent water and food shortages. The next year Crespí accompanied Fages in an attempt to find a route around San Francisco Bay to Port Regis.

By far one of his most successful voyages was the one he embarked on near the end of his life. Well into his 50s, in 1774 Crespí joined an expedition run by Juan Perez that traveled north along the western coast.

As diarist on the journey, Crespí described his initial reluctance to join, saying, "While I was minister of the mission of San Carlos de Monterey, the reverend father president Fray Junípero Serra appointed me to go with the sea expedition and not withstanding that I was much fatigued with so many journeys by land, I made the sacrifice of going on this enterprise, resigning myself to obedience and expecting through God every success in the voyage."

Success was as much a part of that journey as the rugged landscape of the northwestern coast and the icy waters of the North Pacific. The trip expanded Spanish territory into what is now Oregon and Washington. Indeed Crespí was one of the first Europeans to see Washington's Mount Olympus, and he wrote about the fateful day when "the sun appeared and we saw to the east a very high peak, distant from us about eighteen leagues and it seemed to us that it had red spots that looked like cliffs. Some said that it was snow or a hill near the beach with great sand dunes. . . . [W]e drew near again to the land and the high peak covered with snow was plainly visible."

During the expedition Perez explored much of the northwestern coast, including the islands off British Columbia, along with much of Washington and Oregon. "He had given his nation whatever of credit and territorial claims may be founded on the mere act of first discovery," H. H. Bancroft noted in his *History of the Northwest Coast.*

In 1781 Crespí and Serra traveled to visit Palóu in San Francisco. By then the missions in southern Alta California had been handed over to Dominican friars, so Palóu had traveled northward.

Along the coast of San Francisco Bay, the diarist looked over the waters he'd seen a decade before. A short time later, he returned to Carmel. He died on the first day of 1782—he was 60 years old.

But his work lived on. The trail he'd helped establish— El Camino Real—became the route of choice for California travelers for over a century. The mission site he first imagined grew as well.

Mission San Diego was the first permanent European settlement in Alta California, but by the 1770s the location in what would become Los Angeles had gained favor as well. When a new viceroy, Felip de Neve, was elected in California, he discussed Crespí's recommendations with his counterpart in Mexico. The two men agreed that the site by the Los Angeles River was ideal for a settlement.

Now a modern city by the sea, San Diego, California began as a mission settlement in the desert.

King Carlos III agreed. Surprisingly, considering the sprawling and haphazard nature of modern Los Angeles, de Neve drew up careful plans for the future city. He designed pueblos, fields, and pastures. It was probably the first planned community in North America.

Despite his efforts, it was nearly impossible to convince Europeans to settle there. On September 24, 1781, 11 men, 11 women, and 22 children moved into the small adobe houses along the Los Angeles River's shoreline. Boasting glassless windows and doors constructed from rawhide, the homes were simple even for the times. The streets flooded whenever it rained.

Because of those challenges, 20 years later the population had grown to only 300 people.

The Catholic Church had its own difficulties convincing missionaries to risk moving to the New World. A short while after Crespí's death, Palóu and Serra were talking about how tough it was finding missionaries willing to travel to the New World. "If the friars of our Holy Province who knew the late Fray Juan Crespí could but see what he accomplished, and the great harvest which he was able to gather, great numbers of them would be encouraged to come," Serra remarked. "If they were but to read his diaries it would be enough to move many of them to the point of leaving fatherland and monastery to undertake this journey in order to have a share in this vineyard of the Lord."

Spain had a difficult time convincing settlers to relocate to Alta and Baja California. Worse, supply problems continued to plague the settlers, and even with the priests on their side, the native people were often treated cruelly by the soldiers. As a result many Indians died from harsh treatment. Others died from disease.

In the late 18th century, Spain and the mission priests fought over control of the settlements. Spain embarked on a process called secularization, which meant that the settlements would no longer be run by the fathers. Instead the government would operate them. In 1813 the Spanish government issued a decree demanding that the priests "cease from the governing and administration of the [mission] property."

After the Mexican revolt and Mexico's independence from Spain in 1821, the new government implemented a similar policy. The native peoples sided with the priests, who had told them that it was a "great evil" for the government to run the church holdings. Many of the Indians took up arms against government officials; others just destroyed the land.

By 1843 half the missions that Serra and Crespí had founded were abandoned, left to decay in the wilds.

On July 7, 1846, during the U.S.-Mexico War, American forces raised the flag of the United States over the mission at Carmel. The war ended two years later, with Mexico ceding 500,000 square miles to the United States—including Alta California. By then the United States controlled the Oregon and Washington territories as well.

Crespí never became as well known as the explorers he described in his journals. But as Herbert Eugene Bolton explained in the foreword to his book *Fray Juan Crespí: Missionary Explorer of the Pacific Coast*, "Crespí was a gentle character, devout Christian, zealous missionary, faithful companion, his peculiar fame will be that of diarist. Of all the men of this half decade, so prolific in frontier expansion up the Pacific Coast by sea and land, Crespí alone participated in all the major path-breaking expeditions. . . . In distance he out traveled [explorer Francisco Vásquez de] Coronado."

Crespí explored nearly 2,000 miles of the North American landscape and made sea voyages along the coast that were at least twice as long. Even better, he recorded all of those amazing journeys, leaving a detailed record for future generations.■

CHRONOLOGY

1721   born in Majorca, Spain

1730s enters the Franciscan Order

1740s enters University of La Palma

1749   after a dangerous voyage, arrives in North America; travels to Mexico City to the College of San Fernando

1750   travels with Fray Junípero Serra to the mission at Sierra Gorda

1758   returns to College of San Fernando

1769   joins the expedition headed by Gaspar de Portolá to San Diego, Los Angeles, Monterey, and finally San Francisco Bay

1770   founds the Mission San Carlos Borroméo in Monterey

1771   moves mission to Carmel-by-the-Sea, California, and settles there

1774   is made chaplain of expedition to North Pacific

1782   dies January 1 in Carmel

1927   author and historian H. E. Bolton publishes Juan Crespí's diaries in the book *Fray Juan Crespí: Missionary Explorer of the Pacific Coast 1769–1774*

TIMELINE IN HISTORY

1608   The city of Quebec (Canada) is founded by Frenchman Samuel de Champlain.

1620   The *Mayflower* sails from England to North America.

1664   British vessels sail into the Dutch-controlled harbors of New Amsterdam, and after a brief confrontation take over the city—renaming it New York.

1690   The Battle of Boyne in Ireland concludes with a British victory.

1703   Czar Peter the Great founds the city of St. Petersburg in Russia; he will lead his country into greater exploration.

1732   Benjamin Franklin's first *Poor Richard's Almanack* is published.

1739   The War of Jenkins's Ear is waged between England and Spain over control of trade with North America.

1756   The Seven Years' War, also known as the French and Indian War, begins.

1763   After its loss in the Seven Years' War, France gives Canada and all territory east of the Mississippi to England.

1767   The Mason-Dixon Line is established between Maryland and Pennsylvania.

1769   Daniel Boone explores a route through the Cumberland Gap to Kentucky.

1770   British troops kill five in the Boston Massacre.

1773   The Sons of Liberty protest British import taxes by dumping imported tea in Boston Harbor (Boston Tea Party).

1775   The American Revolution begins with battles at Lexington and Concord.

1776   The Declaration of Independence is signed.

1781   The first European settlers arrive in Los Angeles.

1783   Paris peace treaty ends the American Revolution.

1789   The storming of the Bastille Prison in Paris initiates the French Revolution.

1798   An Irish revolt against the British fails.

1804   Meriwether Lewis and William Clark leave St. Louis, embarking on an exploration of the Louisiana Territory, which will greatly expand United States' knowledge of the West.

1812   After British interference in U.S. trade and impressing American seaman into British service, the United States declares war on Britain.

1821   Mexico wins independence from Spain.

1836   Americans settling in the Mexican-controlled province of Texas win their independence.

1848   The United States gains California and New Mexico.

1849   The California gold rush begins.

FOR FURTHER READING

Doherty, Kieran. *Explorers, Missionaries and Trappers.* Minneapolis: The Oliver Press, Inc., 2000.

Hatt, Christine. *The American West: Native Americans, Pioneers and Settlers.* New York: Peter Bedric Books, 1998.

Podell, Janet, and Steven Anzouin. *Old Worlds to New.* New York: The H.H. Wilson Company, 1993.

Smith, Carter, editor. *The Conquest of the West.* Brookfield, Conn.: The Millbrook Press, 1992.

———. *Exploring the Frontier.* Brookfield, Conn.: The Millbrook Press, 1992.

ON THE WEB

California Mission Studies Association
www.ca-missions.org

The California Missions Site
www.californiamissions.com

Carmel Mission Home Page
www.carmelmission.org

San Diego Historical Society
www.sandiegohistory.org

Works Consulted:

1,000 Makers of the Millennium. London: DK Publishing, 1999.

Bancroft, Hubert Howe. *History of the Northwest Coast*. San Francisco: Bancroft and Co., 1884.

Bolton, Herbert Eugene. *Fray Juan Crespí: Missionary Explorer of the Pacific Coast 1769–1774*. Berkeley: University of California Press, 1927.

Bolton, Herbert. *The Spanish Borderlands*. New Haven: The Yale University Press, 1921.

Hill, Kathleen Thompson, and Gerald N. Hill. *Monterey and Carmel: Eden by the Sea*. 2nd edition. Old Saybrook, Conn.: Globe Pequot Press, 2001.

GLOSSARY

alta (ALL-tuh) - Spanish word meaning "upper"

baja (BA-ha) - Spanish word meaning "lower"

conquistadores (kon-KEES-teh-door-eez) - Spanish for "conquerors," the men who used violence to take over territory for the Spanish

cuirassier (KWIR-uh-sir) - a cavalry soldier wearing defensive armor for the torso comprising a breastplate and back plate, originally made of leather

Ice Age - the period beginning 1.6 million years ago and lasting until 11,000 years ago when much of Earth was frozen

league (LEEG) - a unit of measure that varies from 2.4 to 4.6 miles

missionary - a representative of a religious group sent to teach others about that group's religion

missions - church or settlement areas where missionaries convert and educate native peoples

New World - North, South, and Central America. (The "Old World" was whatever was known to Europeans in the 15th century)

presidio (preh-SEE-dee-oh) - headquarters of military authorities

proselytize (PRAH-sleh-tize) - to persuade someone to convert to one's own religion

pueblo (PWEH-blow) - a multilevel adobe building surrounded by an open plaza; also, Indian tribes such as the Hopi who lived in these types of buildings

scurvy (SKUR-vee) - an often fatal disease caused by a lack of vitamin C (found mainly in citrus fruits such as oranges and lemons) that causes bleeding beneath the skin and weakness

viceroy (VICE-roy) - a governor in a country ruled by a king or other sovereign

INDEX